W9-ADN-975

CHL

Come with me on a delightful spree
And enjoy the magic of poetry!

Bobbye S. Goldstein

INNER CHIMES
· POEMS ON POETRY ·

SELECTED BY

BOBBYE S. GOLDSTEIN

ILLUSTRATIONS BY

JANE BRESKIN ZALBEN

WORDSONG

Boyds Mills Press

The artist wishes to acknowledge
Johanna Hurwitz for her encouragement
during this project, and Rachel Fox,
Librarian at the Port Washington Library.

Published by Wordsong / Boyds Mills Press, Inc.
A Highlights Company • 910 Church Street • Honesdale, Pennsylvania 18431

Publisher Cataloging-in-Publication Data
Inner chimes: poems on poetry / edited by Bobbye S. Goldstein;
illustrated by Jane Breskin Zalben.—1st ed.
32 p. : col. ill. ; cm.
Summary: Collected poems which celebrate the creation and wonder of poetry.
1. Children's poetry   [1. Poetry—Collections.]   I. Goldstein, Bobbye S.
II. Zalben, Jane Breskin, ill.   III. Title.   808 / .81—dc20   1992
Library of Congress Catalog Card Number: 92-60040
ISBN 1-56397-040-6

First edition 1992
Book designed by Jane Breskin Zalben
The text of this book was set in Palatino.
The illustrations were done in watercolors.
Distributed by St. Martin's Press
Printed in the United States of America
10   9   8   7   6   5   4   3   2   1

For my husband Gabe and my son Fred
who are always there for me,
and for my mentor and friend Lee Bennett Hopkins.
—B.S.G.

For the three men in my life who provide poetry:
Jonathan, Alexander, and Steven—
where the magic began a quarter of a century ago.
—J.B.Z.

The compiler of *Inner Chimes* and Boyds Mills Press wish to thank the following authors, publishers, and agents for permission to reprint copyrighted material. Every possible effort has been made to trace the ownership of each poem included. If any errors or omissions have occurred, correction will be made in subsequent printings, provided that the publisher is notified of their existence.

"The Poem on My Pillow," by Brod Bagert. Copyright © 1992 by Brod Bagert. Reprinted by permission of the author.

"Days," from BLUE SMOKE by Karle Wilson Baker. Copyright © 1919 by Karle Wilson Baker. Reprinted by permission of Yale University Press.

"Keep A Poem In Your Pocket," from SOMETHING SPECIAL by Beatrice Schenk de Regniers. Copyright © 1958 by Beatrice Schenk de Regniers. Copyright © 1986 renewed. Reprinted by permission of Marian Reiner for the author.

"There Isn't Time," from ELEANOR FARJEON'S POEMS FOR CHILDREN, originally appeared in OVER THE GARDEN WALL by Eleanor Farjeon. Copyright © 1933, 1961 by Eleanor Farjeon. Reprinted by permission of HarperCollins Publishers.

"Poetry," from ELEANOR FARJEON'S POEMS FOR CHILDREN, originally appeared in SING FOR YOUR SUPPER by Eleanor Farjeon. Copyright © 1938 by Eleanor Farjeon; renewed 1966 by Gervase Farjeon. Reprinted by permission of HarperCollins Publishers.

"The Critic," from SONGS FOR JOHNNY JUMP-UP by John Farrar. Registered under Richard R. Smith, Inc. Copyright © 1930. Reprinted by permission of Brandt & Brandt Literary Agents, Inc.

"Because," from COTTON CANDY ON A RAINY DAY by Nikki Giovanni. Copyright © 1978 by Nikki Giovanni. Reprinted by permission of William Morrow & Company, Inc./Publishers, New York.

"The Poem That Got Away," from THE SONG IN MY HEAD by Felice Holman. Copyright © 1985 by Felice Holman. Reprinted by permission of Charles Scribner's Sons, an imprint of Macmillan Publishing Company.

"Poetry Time" by Lee Bennett Hopkins. Copyright © 1992 by Lee Bennett Hopkins. Reprinted by permission of Curtis Brown, Ltd.

"Poems," by Bobbi Katz. Copyright © 1992 by Bobbi Katz. Printed by permission of the author.

"Paperclips," from THE KITE THAT BRAVED OLD ORCHARD BEACH, by X.J. Kennedy. Copyright © 1991 by X.J. Kennedy. Reprinted by permission of Margaret K. McElderry Books, an imprint of Macmillan Publishing Company.

"Unfolding Bud," by Naoshi Koriyama. Copyright © 1957 by The Christian Science Publishing Society. Reprinted by permission from *The Christian Science Monitor*. All rights reserved.

"Take a Word Like Cat," and "Where Do You Get the Idea for a Poem?," from DOGS AND DRAGONS, TREES AND DREAMS by Karla Kuskin. Copyright © 1980 by Karla Kuskin. Reprinted by permission of HarperCollins Publishers.

"Writers," from HEY WORLD, HERE I AM! by Jean Little. Copyright © 1989 by Jean Little. Reprinted by permission of HarperCollins Publishers.

"Shallow Poem," by Gerda Mayer. Copyright © 1970 by Gerda Mayer. First published in AMBIT, 1971. Reprinted by permission of the author.

"Inside a Poem," from A SKY FULL OF POEMS by Eve Merriam. Copyright © 1964, 1970, 1973 by Eve Merriam. Reprinted by permission of Marian Reiner for the author.

"Poets Go Wishing," from POETS GO WISHING by Lilian Moore. Copyright © 1975 by Lilian Moore. Reprinted by permission of Marian Reiner for the author.

"Feelings about Words," from WORDS WORDS WORDS by Mary O'Neill. Copyright © 1966 by Mary O'Neill. Reprinted by permission of Doubleday, a division of Bantam Doubleday Dell Publishing Group, Inc.

"I'm Sitting Writing Poems," by Jack Prelutsky. Copyright © 1991 by Jack Prelutsky. Reprinted by permission of the author.

Contents

Inside a Poem / *Eve Merriam* 1

Poetry / *Eleanor Farjeon* 2

There Isn't Time / *Eleanor Farjeon* 3

Take a Word Like Cat / *Karla Kuskin* 4

Where Do You Get the Idea for a Poem? / *Karla Kuskin* 5

Poets Go Wishing / *Lilian Moore* 6

Unfolding Bud / *Naoshi Koriyama* 7

Feelings about Words / *Mary O'Neill* 8

Writers / *Jean Little* 10

The Poem That Got Away / *Felice Holman* 12

Days / *Karle Wilson Baker* 13

Poems / *Bobbi Katz* 14

Because / *Nikki Giovanni* 16

Poetry Time / *Lee Bennett Hopkins* 17

Shallow Poem / *Gerda Mayer* 18

Paperclips / *X.J. Kennedy* 19

Keep A Poem In Your Pocket / *Beatrice Schenk de Regniers* 20

I'm Sitting Writing Poems / *Jack Prelutsky* 21

The Poem on My Pillow / *Brod Bagert* 22

The Critic / *John Farrar* 24

Inside a Poem

It doesn't always have to rhyme,
but there's the repeat of a beat, somewhere
an inner chime that makes you want to
tap your feet or swerve in a curve;
a lilt, a leap, a lightning-split:—
thunderstruck the consonants jut,
while the vowels open wide as waves in the noon-
    blue sea.

Eve Merriam

Poetry

What is Poetry? Who knows?
Not a rose, but the scent of the rose;
Not the sky, but the light in the sky;
Not the fly, but the gleam of the fly;
Not the sea, but the sound of the sea;
Not myself, but what makes me
See, hear, and feel something that prose
Cannot: and what it is, who knows?

Eleanor Farjeon

There Isn't Time

There isn't time, there isn't time
    To do the things I want to do—
With all the mountain tops to climb
    And all the woods to wander through
And all the seas to sail upon,
    And everywhere there is to go,
And all the people, every one,
    Who live upon the earth to know.
There's only time, there's only time
    To know a few, and do a few,
And then sit down and make a rhyme
    About the rest I want to do.

Eleanor Farjeon

Take a Word Like Cat

Take a word like cat
And build around it;
A fur room over here
A long meow
Floating from the chimney like a smoke tail.
Draw with words.
Balance them like blocks.
Carve word furniture:
A jar of pussy willows,
Catkins, phlox,
Milk in a dish,
Catnip pillows,
A silver bell,
A plaster bird,
An eaten fish.
When everything is perfect in its place
Step back to view the home
That you have built of words around your word.
It is a poem.

Karla Kuskin

Where Do You Get the Idea for a Poem?

Where do you get the idea for a poem?
Pippety
Poppety
Peep.
Does it shake you awake?
Do you dream it asleep?
Or into your tiny tin head does it creep
And pop from your pen when you are not aware
Or leap from your pocket
Or fall from your hair
Or is it just silently
Suddenly
There?
In a beat
In a breath
In a pause
In a cry
One unblinking eye
That stares from the dark
That is deep in your head
Demanding attention
Until it is written
Until it is rotten
Until it is anything else but forgotten
Until it is read.

Karla Kuskin

Poets Go Wishing

Poets go fishing
with buckets
of words,
fishing
and wishing.

Using a line
that's loose or
tight
(Maybe this time
a rhyme is
right.)

Unreeling
unreeling
the words till they
match
the feeling the poet is
trying to
catch.

Lilian Moore

Unfolding Bud

One is amazed
By a water-lily bud
Unfolding
With each passing day,
Taking on a richer color
And new dimensions.

One is not amazed,
At first glance,
By a poem,
Which is as tight-closed
As a tiny bud.

Yet one is surprised
To see the poem
Gradually unfolding,
Revealing its rich inner self
As one reads it
Again
And over again.

Naoshi Koriyama

Feelings about Words

Some words clink
As ice in drink.
Some move with grace
A dance, a lace.
Some sound thin:
Wail, scream and pin.
Some words are squat:
A mug, a pot,
And some are plump,
Fat, round and dump.
Some words are light:
Drift, lift and bright.
A few are small:
A, is and all.
And some are thick,
Glue, paste and brick.
Some words are sad:
"I never had . . . ."
And others gay:
Joy, spin and play.
Some words are sick:
Stab, scratch and nick.

Some words are hot:
Fire, flame and shot.
Some words are sharp,
Sword, point and carp.
And some alert:
Glint, glance and flirt.
Some words are lazy:
Saunter, hazy.
And some words preen:
Pride, pomp and queen.
Some words are quick,
A jerk, a flick.
Some words are slow:
Lag, stop and grow,
While others poke
As ox with yoke.
Some words can fly—
There's wind, there's high:
And some words cry:
"Goodbye . . .
Goodbye . . . ."

Mary O'Neill

QUEEN PRIDE POMP JOY

SWORD FLICK JERK ice

HIGH

small A

HAZY Wind slow POINT glance

sratch

dance drift lift flir

mug pot

STOP STAB

round

lace grow

SCREAM

WAIL

FIRE!

azy

spin

FLAME

glint

BRIGHT

NICK

play BRICK glue paste

Goodbye...

Writers

Emily writes of poetic things
Like crocuses and hummingbirds' wings,
But I think people beat hummingbirds every time.

Emily likes to write of snow
And dawn and candlelight aglow,
But I'd rather write about me and Emily and stuff like that.

The funny thing is, I delight
To read what Emily likes to write,
And Emily says she thinks my poems are okay too.

Also, sometimes, we switch with each other.
Emily writes of a fight with her mother.
I tell about walking alone by the river,
     —how still and golden it was.

I know what Emily means, you see,
And, often, Emily's halfway me . . .
Oh, there's just no way to make anybody else understand.

We're not a bit the same and yet,
We're closer than most people get.
There's no one word for it. We just care about each other
     the way we are supposed to.

So I can look through Emily's eyes
And she through mine. It's no surprise,
When you come right down to it, that we're friends.

Jean Little

The Poem That Got Away

There I was and in it came
Through the fogbank of my brain
From the fastness of my soul
Shining like a glowing coal—
The nearly perfect poem!

Oh, it may have needed just
An alteration here or there—
A little tuck, a little seam
to be exactly what I mean—
The really perfect poem!

I'll write it later on, I said,
The idea's clear and so's my head.
This pen I have is nearly dry.
What I'll do now is finish this pie,
Then on to the perfect poem!

With pen in hand quite full of ink
I try now to recall.
I've plenty of time in which to think
But the poem went down the kitchen sink
With the last of the perfect pie.

Felice Holman

Days

Some days my thoughts are just cocoons—all
    cold and dull and blind,
They hang from dripping branches in the
    grey woods of my mind;
And other days they drift and shine—such
    free and flying things!
I find the gold-dust in my hair, left by
    their brushing wings.

Karle Wilson Baker

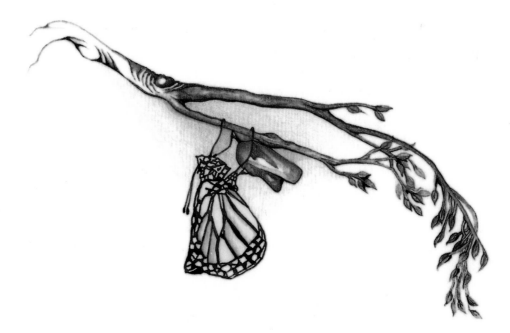

Poems

A poem is a magical boat to ride
in a sea of words with a rhyming tide.
It takes us from some hum-drum shore
to places we never have been before—
shimmering islands of sensation
captured by imagination.
New lands wait for us to sight,
so climb aboard! The wind is right.
Rocking rhythms will take us along
to the rising crest of a noteless song.

Bobbi Katz

Because

i wrote a poem
for you because
you are
my little boy

i wrote a poem
for you because
you are
my darling daughter

and in this poem
i sang a song
that says
as time goes on
i am you
and you are me
and that's how life
goes on

Nikki Giovanni

Poetry Time

It's poem o'clock.
Time for a rhyme—

tick-tock
ding-dong
bing-bong
or
chime.

Poems are

wistful
wish-filled
sublime—

Come.

Unlock a minute
for
poetry time.

Lee Bennett Hopkins

Shallow Poem

I've thought of a poem.
I carry it carefully,
nervously, in my head,
like a saucer of milk;
in case I should spill some lines
before I can put it down.

Gerda Mayer

Paperclips

A jumbled sight,
The sheets I write!
    High time for paperclips
To take a bite
And grip them tight
    Between bright bulldog lips.

X.J. Kennedy

Keep A Poem In Your Pocket

Keep a poem in your pocket
and a picture in your head
and you'll never feel lonely
at night when you're in bed.

The little poem will sing to you
the little picture bring to you
a dozen dreams to dance to you
at night when you're in bed.

So—
Keep a picture in your pocket
and a poem in your head
and you'll never feel lonely
at night when you're in bed.

Beatrice Schenk de Regniers

I'm Sitting Writing Poems

I'm sitting writing poems in the middle
     of the night,
I've yet to sleep a wink.
There's something telling me to write
The magic that I think.

My lamp is lit, my eyes are wide,
I've put off counting sheep.
Unless I get my thoughts outside,
I'll never fall asleep.

My pencil sings as words take wing,
I shiver with delight.
My favorite amazing thing
Is sitting writing poems in the middle
     of the night.

Jack Prelutsky

The Poem on My Pillow

I felt very small
And the house was dark
But those cookies kept calling from the kitchen
So I tiptoed downstairs
And peeked around the corner
To make sure there were no monsters.

Then I saw my dad
Alone at the kitchen table
With an open book
And a pencil and paper.
He wrote very carefully,
Then he stopped and listened . . .
And he smiled.

This morning I found this poem on my pillow.

To the Little Boy Who Hides

I listen for your breath while you sleep.
I follow your footsteps across the floor above me.
I hear the creek of wooden steps as you tiptoe down.
And I feel your fear of darkness.
Oh little son,
You need not hide from the night.
Speak out . . .
Your courage will make light.

When I read the poem I thought
My gosh . . . he heard me!
Was he angry?
Did he think I had been bad?
Then I noticed how he signed the poem . . .

To My Son . . . With Love . . . from Dad.

Brod Bagert

The Critic

Sometimes when it is bedtime,
My mother comes to me,
She takes me from my warm bed,
And sits me on her knee.

And it is very pleasant
To hear her golden voice,
Reading bedtime stories
According to my choice.

And when she reads me poems,
The kind that I like best—
The music of them lulls me
Quite gently to my rest.

Now, often when I'm wakeful
I count a million sheep—
But poems are far, far better
For putting kids to sleep.

John Farrar